FAN-MAIL

by the same author

criticism
THE METROPOLITAN CRITIC
VISIONS BEFORE MIDNIGHT
(Jonathan Cape Ltd)

verse published by Jonathan Cape Ltd
with illustrations by Russell Davies
PEREGRINE PRYKKE'S PILGRIMAGE THROUGH THE LONDON
LITERARY WORLD

with illustrations by Marc
THE FATE OF FELICITY FARK IN THE LAND OF THE
MEDIA
BRITANNIA BRIGHT'S BEWILDERMENT IN THE WILDERNESS
OF WESTMINSTER

collections of lyrics set and sung by Pete Atkin on the
RCA label
BEWARE OF THE BEAUTIFUL STRANGER
DRIVING THROUGH MYTHICAL AMERICA
A KING AT NIGHTFALL
THE ROAD OF SILK
SECRET DRINKER
THE RIDER TO THE WORLD'S END
LIVE LIBEL
THE MASTER OF THE REVELS

song-book written with Pete Atkin and published by
Warner Bros Music Ltd
A FIRST FOLIO

Fan-Mail

SEVEN VERSE LETTERS

Clive James

FABER AND FABER
3 Queen Square London

First published in 1977
by Faber and Faber Limited
3 Queen Square London WC1
Printed in Great Britain by
The Bowering Press Limited
Plymouth

ISBN 0 571 11058 4

to Russell Davies

CONTENTS

Foreword   11

To Russell Davies: a letter from Cardiff   13

To John Fuller: a letter from London   22

To Martin Amis: a letter from Indianapolis   28

To Pete Atkin: a letter from Paris   37

To Prue Shaw: a letter from Cambridge   45

To Tom Stoppard: a letter from London   52

To Peter Porter: a letter to Sydney   57

FOREWORD

I wrote the first five of these seven verse letters in 1974, between finishing *Peregrine Prykke's Pilgrimage* (a scurrilous mock epic, confected from rhyming couplets, which I have since revised and expanded) and beginning *The Fate of Felicity Fark* (another mock epic, equally reprehensible and also in couplets, which was completed early in 1975). Later in 1975 I wrote the last two letters, before beginning a third mock epic, *Britannia Bright's Bewilderment*, which appeared in 1976 and turned out to be no more savoury than its predecessors.

Taken as a whole, the verse letters and the first two mock epics constitute a perhaps belated attempt, in my thirty-fifth year (with a few month's latitude either side), to discipline technique by running the gamut of the set forms – or part of the gamut, anyway. A pious enough aim, which I hope cheerfulness has done something to mollify, since keeping to strict rules is a pleasure as well as a challenge. I need hardly say that the reader is meant to forge on unperturbed by technical considerations, but those interested in these things might like to know that apart from the letter to Tom Stoppard, which is written in my own adaptation of an Audenesque *rime couée* stanza, the forms are as close to standard practice as I can make them. The letter to Russell Davies is in rhyme royal; the letter to John Fuller in Burnsian *rime couée*; the letter to Martin Amis in Spenserian stanza; the letter to Pete Atkin in *ottava rima*; the letter to my wife, Prue Shaw, in *terza rima*; and the letter to Peter Porter in rhyming couplets.

I would like to thank Ian Hamilton for first printing the letter to Pete Atkin in the *New Review*; Anthony Thwaite for setting aside five pages of *Encounter* to publish the letter to Martin Amis; and especially Claire Tomalin, who generously made so much of the *New Statesman's* exiguous space available for the letters to John Fuller, Tom Stoppard and Peter Porter.

Thanks must also go to my wife, whose fastidious ear ensured that my Australian pronunciation (which gives a word like 'cyclist' three syllables and, if I am not careful, a word like 'admiring' four) was not too often foisted on the public as English prosody. The letter to her, like the one to Russell Davies, is here appearing for the first time.

This collection is dedicated to Russell Davies for all the reasons set out in my letter to him, plus an additional one which had not yet fully become clear when that letter was written. In the recitals of my mock epics at the Poetry International Festivals, he has single-handedly incarnated all the scores of different characters, giving me the enviable satisfaction of watching my often meagre notions take on abundant life.

The film alluded to in the letters to Russell Davies and Pete Atkin rejoiced in the title *Barry McKenzie Holds His Own*. It was written by Barry Humphries and Bruce Beresford and directed by Bruce Beresford. Conventions of literary raillery ought not to disguise a profound debt to John Fuller, whose prize-winning volume *Epistles to Several Persons* first aroused my competitive instincts with its convincing demonstration that verse can still hope to be both public and exact.

TO RUSSELL DAVIES:
A LETTER FROM CARDIFF

Dear *Dai* : I'm writing to you from Location
For the new *McKenzie* film, in which I play
A role that would have filled me with elation
When I used to drink two-handed every day,
But as things are, it fills me with dismay –
With me no more than three weeks on the wagon
They're handing me free *Foster's* by the flagon.

I'm meant to be, you see, a drunken Critic
Arrived in *Europe* from the Great South Land :
The least articulate, most paralytic
Plug-ugly in *McKenzie's* merry band,
Escorting that chaste hero on a grand
Excursion through the more arcane and zanier
Interstices of deepest *Transylvania.*

Which place we double here, in *Cardiff (Wales),*
Whose *Burges* follies neatly fill the bill :
They've even got the right-sized drawbridge nails.
Cold *Castle Coch*, perched darkly on a hill,
And *Cardiff Castle* in the city, will,
When cut together, serve as a spectacular
Surround for a Larf Riot spoofing *Dracula.*

Oh *Cardiff! Dai*, your homeland's sovereign seat,
This city of arcades and . . . more arcades,
I've hardly seen yet. Is there a main street?
No time for galleries or bookshop raids:
When precious shooting-time at evening fades
We shuttle back in vans to our hotel
And thank *God* that at least the beds work well

For nothing else there operates at all.
You risk your reason when you take your key.
They never wake you if you leave a call,
Do when you don't, refuse to give you tea
In bed unless asked not to – but get me.
I'm dining every evening in the presence
Of clown *Dick Bentley*, clever *Donald Pleasence*

And crazy *Barry Humphries*: no regrets.
On top of that, of course, I watch them work
Their wonders from sun-rise until it sets –
A feast of practised talent which I lurk
In awe to ogle, feeling like a Berk.
I think, my friend, our highest common factor
The certainty we share that I'm no actor.

Whereas, of course, you are – about the best
I met at *Cambridge*. Have you given up
That gift to spend more effort on the rest?
Your dispositions overflow the cup.
No matter. Early days. The night's a pup.
Though there be times you'd like to see the back of
A few of all those Trades you're such a Jack of

It's too soon to be certain what's dispensable.
You're bound to write more, draw more, play more jazz:
The man who brands your output reprehensible
You'll know to be a monodist like *Bazz*,

Whose one-track mind's the only knack he has.
I fear our purist friends find nothing seedier
Than how we spread ourselves around the Media,

But we both know you are, with all your Bents,
As much compelled as I am with my few
To make from Art and Life some kind of sense
That leaves room for enjoying what we do.
Hermetic rhetoric aside, what's new
In serving more than one urge to excel
Like *Michelangelo* or *Keith Michell?*

Now I myself, though full-time a Pop Lyricist,
Have found the odd stint as a strict-form poet
Has rendered me less trusting, more empiricist,
Concerning Technique and the need to know it.
This stuff you must make work or else you blow it.
Sincere Intent alone is not enough:
For though the Tone is light, the Rules are tough.

The Obstacle, says *Gianfranco Contini*,
Is what brings Creativity to birth.
(His mind unlocks a problem like *Houdini*.
The best-equipped Philologist on *Earth*,
Contini, in my view – for what that's worth –
Was sent by Providence to heal the schism
That sunders Scholarship from Criticism.)

The Obstacle for *Dante*, claims the Prof.,
Lay in the strictness of the *terza rima*.
The old New Style perforce was written off,
Or rather, written up: the lyric dreamer
Got sharper with his tongue, became a schemer
Co-opting dozens of vocabularies
Into a language that forever varies

Yet in its forward pressure never falters –
A rhythmic pulse that somehow stays the same
For all its concrete detail always alters.
A form he would, when young, have thought a game
Had now the status of a sacred flame,
A fertile self-renewing Holy Trinity
Designed to give his *Comedy* divinity.

It worked, too, as I'm sure you have detected
Now that you're trained to read the *Eyetie* tongue.
At least I hope you have. If you've neglected
Your *Dante* when like mine your wife's among
His foremost female fans, you should be hung.
At getting *Alighieri* through to students
Your *Judy*'s letter-perfect, like my *Prudence*.

She's perfect in all ways . . . but I digress.
However true, it's crass to call one's spouse
A paragon of loving comeliness
Who yet rates Alpha Double Plus for nous
While still remaining keen to clean the house.
A paradox worth pondering upon:
We each loathed *Academe*, yet wed a *Don*.

I don't know what my wife's at, half the time:
Locked up with microfilms of some frail text
Once copied from a copy's copy. I'm
Dead chuffed as well as miffed to be perplexed,
Contented neither of us has annexed
The other's field. Though it's conceited-sounding.
We *Jameses* think each other quite astounding.

I'd like to be back there at home right now,
Receiving from my helpmeet a fond look.
But here we Aussies are, rehearsing how
To quell with every cheap trick in the book

The Castle's evil Oriental cook –
A role played by a lithe and slightly spooky
Karate-ka 5th Dan, *Meijii Suzuki.*

He is (ah, but you twigged!) a *Japanese.*
I've never seen a man more fit or fleeter.
That guy can pull your teeth out with his knees
And kick the whiskers off a passing cheetah.
To *Bazza's* pals (me, *Scrotum, Tazz* and *Skeeter*)
Whom *Meijii* smites (the script says) hip and thigh,
He looks like at least Seven *Samurai.*

Perhaps propelled by an electric motor
His flying feet can draw blood like a knife.
His brain by *Sony*, body by *Toyota*,
This bloke's the Yellow Peril to the life:
And yet, a man of Peace. In place of strife
He puts a focused force of meditation
That transcendentalizes Aggravation.

A day of learning not to get too near him
Can leave you breathless. Think I'll hit the sack.
I'd like to tell the lad that, while I fear him,
I love the way he works; but there's a lack
In our Communication. Keeping track
Of when he plans to lash out without warning
Has knackered me for now. More in the morning.

* *

Another day since I began composing
These verses in spare moments has now passed,
And here's a whole free hour I can't spend dozing:
A chance to see the Gallery at last.
It's early closing, though: so, breathing fast,
I sprint to the Museum, pay 10 pee,
Race up the stairs, and Pow! Guess what I see:

Enough to make a man burst into tears.
Renoir's 'Parisian Girl'. A lilting dream
He painted, to the year, one hundred years
Ago. Deep storm-cloud blue and double cream,
Her clothes and skin are eddies in a stream
Of brush-strokes on a shawl of pastel silk,
A peacock-feather spectrum drowned in milk.

These rhapsodies in blue are his best things,
The style in which he really gets it on.
The *Jeu de Paume* has one that fairly sings –
A portrait of his kids, including *Jean*,
The boy who, when *Pierre-Auguste* was gone,
Became *Renoir* – whose pictures, as it proved,
Were just as human, just as great, and moved.

Even unto the second generation
Sheer genius descended, fully-fashioned.
A transference that rates as a sensation:
That kind of baton-change is strictly rationed.
For which our gratitude should be impassioned –
If artistry, like money, ran in blood-lines
You very soon would find those blood-lines dud lines

Or dead lines. But we ought to leave to *P.B.*
Medawar the Nature-Nurture number:
I'm sure he's in the right. I'd get the heebie-
-jeebies reading *Eysenck*, except slumber
Has always supervened. They're loads of lumber,
Those figures meant to prove genetic strains
Determine your inheritance of brains,

For nobody escapes the play of chance.
The contract's binding: you have got the part.
You have to mime and juggle, sing and dance,
And when you think you've got the role by heart

Some idiot rewrites it from the start.
Nor is there, when your scenes run into trouble,
A volunteer prepared to be your double.

Tomorrow we're to film the Kung-Fu brawl.
It's imminence has got me feeling cagey,
Not least because I'm due to take a fall.
I'm worried (a) my acting might look stagey,
And (b) I'll have my head caved in by *Meijii*.
Cavorting with delight at making flicks
He'll get his thrills, but I might get his kicks.

The Fight-Arranger is my chum *Alf Joint*,
The Stunt-Man King (he did '*Where Eagles Dare*',
The caper on the cable-car). The point,
Says *Alf*, in flying safely through the air
Is landing with some energy to spare
So as to ease the shock of logs and boulders
By smart use of one's padded arms and shoulders.

'You're falling about two foot six' they've said.
When put like that it doesn't sound like much.
The catch, though, is I'm landing on my head.
My first film role will need the tumbler's touch
Or else end on a stretcher or a crutch.
From *Alf*, whose done an eighty-times-as-high dive,
I can't expect much sympathy when *I* dive.

This could be the last stanza of my poem.
I'll scrawl a coda if I come up smiling,
But now I have to get out there and show 'em.
I find the idea nowhere near beguiling:

Suzuki's leg looks like a concrete piling.
But Hell, let's go. What's coping with a killer
To someone who wrote monthly for *Karl Miller*?

* *

Per ardua ad astra. I survived!
The scrap went perfectly. In *Panavision*
It should seem like the Day of Wrath's arrived.
My nose and *Meijii*'s toe faked their collision
And I, without a second's indecision,
Collapsed. I toast (in *Coke*) Success (comparative)
And him who wrote my role into the narrative,

Bruce Beresford. From birth, my oldest mate
Was destined to call 'Action', 'Cut' and 'Print'
And 'Stop' and 'What went wrong? You fainted late',
'You died too soon,' 'No good, I saw you squint'
And (this to me) 'You're mugging. Make like *Clint*
Or *Kirk* or *Burt*. Don't even bat an eyelid:
Then, when the kick comes, crumple the way I did.'

That we would see in letters five feet high
His name one day spread shining in the gloom
Preceded with the words 'Directed by' –
To doubt that prospect there was never room.
He had the screenplay ready in the womb.
He was (he'll know I say it without unction)
By Nature built for one Creative Function.

Alas, not true for us. We're several-sided;
I to a certain, you to a large, degree.
The age is vanished when we might have prided
Ourselves on that. *Karl Marx* said History
Will get a re-run, but as Parody.
The Universal Man won't be returning.
Too bad. But as I write, the Castle's burning:

Our week in *Wales* will finish with this shot.
The clapper-board has clapped it's final clap.
Sighs. Tears. Farewells. You know the bit. The lot.
We'll soon hear, barring unforeseen mishap,
The First Assistant calling 'It's a wrap.'
Of our last day, this is the day's last light
When darkest daylight shades to lightest night –

The time the film-crew calls the Golden Hour.
The Castle quakes. The FX flames leap higher.
We rescue *Edna Everage* from the Tower
And super the End Titles on the fire.
The Heavy croaks. Our triumph is entire.
It's time to say 'Nuff said'. You don't mind, do you?
I'll post this now, then try to beat it to you.

TO JOHN FULLER:
A LETTER FROM LONDON

John Fuller, though we haven't as yet
In the narrow how-do-you-do sense met,
You heard me lose in a verbal set-
   -to early this Winter
A wrangle I should sooner forget
   With *Harold Pinter.*

Unfit for struggling through the press
Afterwards with a view to es-
-tablishing rapport, I'm less
   Distraught today,
And so with sang-froid if not finesse
   Let me roundly say

How deucedly much I have enjoyed
Your bundle of verse letters*, buoyed
Up by the skill you have employed,
   Your *Herrlichkeit*:
Your tongue is platinum unalloyed –
   Like, you can write.

Your form's from *Burns*, plus the brio *Auden*
Praised when he addressed *George Gordon*
Lord Byron: in you, all three co-ordin-
   -ate their roles.
With, I'm afraid, a whiff of the *Warden*
   Of All Souls.

* *Epistles to Several Persons*, by John Fuller.

But the speed, the grace, *che sprezzatura*!
It goes like a rabbit drawn by *Dürer*.
I risk, in trying to ape so pure a
    Style, mockery:
There ain't no kudos for bravura
    If one drops the crockery.

But a cat may look at a king. Though you
And I are in no way spiritu-
-ally allied like the younger *Schu-*
    -bert and *Rossini*,
We're as closely meshed in at least one view
    As the *Arnolfini*.

You like Art it takes *nous* to make
And can't quite, even for pity's sake,
Smile when a dolt thinks he's being *Blake*
    By just doing his thing.
However sincere, the Crass is Fake –
    That's the song you sing.

Right on. Small wonder, then, that *James
Fenton*'s eyes throw gem-like flames:
He matches you in these verse-form games
    Strophe for strophe.
The boy's so quick I suspect his name's
    On the *Schneider Trophy*.

All that *Mirandolan* erudition!
An exophthalmic Man-With-A-Mission
(The wits of *Trotsky*, the looks of *Titian*),
    He's bound to get famous.
He's a lengthened, scholarly edition
    Of *Martin Amis*.

And *Ian Hamilton* gets your blessing.
Saying how I agree would entail digressing
For fifteen pages, as well as confessing
   My depth of debt –
Which to see declared he would find distressing,
   On that I'd bet.

So let's just say that you've sent a letter
To *guru numero uno*. Better
Minds there may be but I've not met a
   Single example.
(The dunces, victims of his vendetta,
   Would say none's ample.)

At *The Pillars of Hercules*, in the bar,
He holds his court, half monk, half Czar,
Reminding his men true letters are
   Not mere marked paper
But a much more life-and-death by far
   Species of caper.

Reminding *you*, too, *John* : for I
Reluctantly must identify
Such apogees of Look-Ma-I'm-Fly-
   -ing in these pages
That despite their enchantment for ear and eye
   My spirit rages.

Fascination of what's difficult?
OK, but why this terrific cult
For stanzas pressure-packed like a mult-
   -iple *M1* pile-up?
Is the aim to bring, as a vivid result,
   The reader's bile up?

Your *French* and *Latin*, with the aid of cribs,
He might just manage, but his schooling jibs
At *Welsh*, for Christ's sake! Come on, no fibs:
   Are you a *Druid*?
Or a second-home Don with the yen (and dibs)
   For vacs unsewered?

To *insist* on being misunderstood –
What an *Oxford* conception of the good!
This book's as twisted as *Hollywood*,
   Only in reverse:
In some departments bent, I should
   Say, even worse.

Bereft of sweetness and of light
Mass Man, you gaily mourn, has blight
For Art: for Life, perpetual night.
   In your gloomy joy
You sound up-tight and out of sight
   Like your father *Roy*.

Odi profanum, chaps! *Il conto*,
Per favore. The West is dying, *Tonto*.
Fit though few at the Hellespont, '*Au-*
   -x armes!' they cry –
αιει δε πυραι νεκυων καιοντο
   θαμειαι.

You've made today, *John*, a special day
In my Year of Changes – the middle way
Of life. Superbly you've had your say
   And should take pride
In putting so splendidly on display
   What I can't abide.

What Art *should* be, there is no knowing
(It's a no-no question *Twits* keep throwing);
But *I* like things that, while never going
    Against the facts
Are as unselfconscious as *Flagstad* sewing
    Between the acts.

For *Ian* and you, in the same small boat
Feeding the crocodiles in the moat
That rings *Parnassus*, I still would vote
    If called upon :
Keeping that coracle always afloat
    Is a *sine qua non.*

But *my* claims to the peak I dump
This day forever, and on my rump
Go bouncing down to stop with a bump
    In one *Hell* of a place
Where I'm hit in the head by the blood-pump thump
    Of a *Fender* bass.

Gut Rock! No plumes of loveliness
Like the *Laudate Dominum* of the *Ves-*
-perae solennes de confess-
    -ore, no :
But another, for me as interes-
    -ting, story though.

Gut Rock! No perfumed interplay
Of *Berlioz* and *Gautier*
Like what goes on in *Les Nuits d'Été.*
    No *Wolf* or *Schumann.*
No *Poulenc, Strauss, Duparc, Fauré* –
    Just *Randy Newman.*

But he'll do. *John,* down here the Truth
Survives. That whoring after Youth
Is a sure-fire way to blow my couth
   You needn't warn
(Ich habe Heimweh as bad as *Ruth*
   In the alien corn)

And how cardio-cerebral growths like Art
Are dialogues between Mind and Heart,
On that we agree – but where we part-
   -'s over your conviction
They natter together like *Beauvoir* and *Sart-*
   -re, in *Mandarin* diction.

Well, I think that's just about it.
I've dug the dirt, I've slung the . . . Bit
By bit I've squandered my penn'orth of wit
   In this Verse Epistle :
The secret is knowing when to quit.
   Time to blow the whistle

And bellow SON, IT'S A BRILLIANT BOOK!
(I'd have been more cheeky than you might brook
Had I said, while spurning the path you took,
   That this stuff you do
Can't be as clever as you make it look
   If I can do it too.)

TO MARTIN AMIS:
A LETTER FROM INDIANAPOLIS

Dear *Mart*, I write you from a magic spot.
The dullsville capital of *Indiana*
At this one point, for this one day, has got
Intensity in every nut and spanner.
Soon now the cars will sing their vast Hosannah
And Pressure will produce amazing Grace.
Drake-Offenhauser! A. J. Foyt's bandanna!
Velazquez painting *Philip* at the chase
Saw something like these colours, nothing like this Race.

Ten-thirty. Half an hour before the start.
The press-box at the *Brickyard* is up high.
We sit here safely, Emperors set apart,
And kibbitz down as Those About to Die
Cry '*Morituri* . . .' Yes, but so am I,
And so are you, though not now. When we're older.
Where Death will be the last thing we defy,
These madmen feel it perching on their shoulder:
The tremble of the heat is tinged with something colder.

But that's enough of talk about the weather.
To rail against the climate's not good form.
My subject ought to be the latest feather
Protruding from your cap. I mean the *Maugham*.
I offer you, through gritted teeth, my warm

Congratulations on another *coup*.
Success for you's so soon become the norm,
Your fresh young ego might be knocked askew.
A wide-spread fear, I find. Your father thinks so too.

The prize's terms dictate an expedition
To distant lands. That makes you Captain *Kirk*
Of Starship *Enterprise*. Your Five-Year Mission :
Exploring Unknown Worlds. You mustn't shirk
The challenge. This Award's not just a perk :
Queer *Maugham*'s £500 are meant to send
Your mind in search of fodder for your Work
Through any far-flung way you care to wend.
Which means, at present rates, a fortnight in *Southend*,

So choosing *Andalusia* took nerve.
It's certainly some kind of Foreign Part.
A bit close-flung, perhaps, but it will serve
To show you the left knee, if not the heart,
Of European Culture. It's a start.
Like *Chesterfield* advising his young son
(Who didn't, I imagine, give a fart)
I'm keen to see your life correctly run.
You can't just arse around forever having *fun*.

The day's work here began at 6 a.m.
The first car they pumped full of gasoline
And wheeled out looked unworldly, like a LEM.
A Mass was said. 'The *Lord* is King.' The scene
Grew crammed with every kind of clean machine.
An *Offenhauser* woke with shrieks and yells.
The heart-throb *Dayglo* pulse and *Duco* preen
Of decals filled the view with charms and spells
As densely drawn and brilliant as the *Book of Kells*.

BORG WARNER. BARDAHL. 'Let the Earth Rejoice.'
'May *Christ* Have Mercy.' LODESTAR. OLSONITE.
America exults with sponsored voice
From *Kitty Hawk* to ultra-Lunar flight.
RAYBESTOS. GULF. Uptight and out of sight!
The *Cape*. BELL HELMETS. *Gemini*. *Apollo!*
Jay Gatsby put his faith in the Green Light.
Behold his dream, and who shall call it hollow?
What genius they have, what destinies they follow!

The big Pre-Race Parade comes down the straight
While hardened press-men lecherously dote
On schoolgirl Majorettes all looking great
In boots and spangled swimsuits. Flags denote
Their provenance. The band from *Terre Haute*
Is called the *Marching Patriots*. *Purdue*
Have got a drum so big it needs a float.
And now the *Dancing Bears* come prancing through,
Their derrières starred white and striped with red and blue.

From *Tucson*, *Kokomo* and *Tuscaloosa*,
From over the State Line and far away,
Purveying the complete *John Philip Sousa*
The kids have come for this one day in *May*
To show the watching world the *U.S.A.*
Survives and thrives and still knows how to cock its
Snoot. Old *Uncle Sam* is A-OK –
He's strutting with bright buttons and high pockets.
Hail, *Tiger Band* from *Circleville! Broad Ripple Rockets!*

Objectively, perhaps, they *do* look tatty.
This continent's original invaders
Were not, however, notably less ratty.
Torpedoes in tin hats and leather waders,
Hard bastards handing beads around like traders –

Grand larceny in every squeak and rattle.
The whole deal was a nightmare of *Ralph Nader*'s,
A corporate racket dressed up as a battle:
The locals kissed the *Spaniard*'s foot or died like cattle.

The choice between the New World and the Old
I've never found that clear, to tell the truth.
Tradition? Yes indeed, to that I hold:
These bouncing brats from *Des Moines* and *Duluth*
Seem short of every virtue except Youth.
But really, was there that much more appeal
In stout *Cortez*'s lack of ruth and couth
Simply because it bore the Papal seal?
It's Art that makes the difference, and Art means the Ideal:

Velazquez (vide supra) for example.
You're visiting the *Prado*, I presume?
Well, when you do, you'll find a healthy sample
Abstracted from his *œuvre* from womb to tomb.
The key works line one giant, stunning room:
Group portraits done in and around the Court
Whose brilliance cleans your brains out like a broom.
Bravura, yes. But products, too, of Thought:
An inner world in which the Kings ruled as they ought,

Not as they did. His purpose wasn't flattery
Or cravenly to kiss the Royal rod.
He just depicted the assault and battery
Of *Hapsburg* policies as acts of *God*,
Whose earthly incarnation was the clod
That currently inhabited the Throne.
He deified the whole lot on his tod,
Each Royal no-no, nincompoop and crone.
Great *Titian* was long gone. *Velazquez* was alone.

Alone, and hemmed about by mediocrities
(Except for once when *Rubens* came to town),
He must have felt as singular as *Socrates*
But didn't let the pressure get him down.
He slyly banked his credit with the Crown
Until he was allowed a year abroad
(In *Rome*, of course. In *Venice* he might drown.)
To raise his sights by study. An award
The *King* well knew would be a hundredfold restored.

Conquistadores in their *armadura*
The drivers now are standing by their cars.
Unholy soldiers (but in purpose purer),
They look as if they're shipping out for *Mars*.
It's hard to tell the Rookies from the Stars :
When suited-up and masked, they seem the same.
White skin-grafts are the veteran's battle-scars.
For *A. J. Foyt* the searing price of Fame
Was branded round his mouth the day he ate the Flame.

A year back young *Swede Savage* swallowed fire.
He took six months to die. It goes to show
How hot it is inside a funeral pyre
And just how hard a row the drivers hoe.
I can't believe they're in this for the dough.
The secret's not beyond, but *in*, the Fear :
A focal point of Grief they get to know
Some other place a million miles from here –
The dream *Hart Crane* once had, to Travel in a Tear.

Eleven on the dot. The Zoo gets hit
By lightning. Lions whelp and panthers panic.
The fastest qualifiers quit the pit
No more than hipbone-high to a mechanic
And take the track. The uproar is Satanic.

By now the less exalted have departed,
But still the sound is monumental, manic.
Librarians would hear it broken-hearted.
And this lap's just for lining up. They haven't started.

Around the Speedway cruising on the Ton
(Which means for *Indy* cars, they're nearly stalling)
They blaze away like spaceships round the Sun –
A shout of thunder like *Valhalla* falling.
(I'm running out of epithets: it's galling.
I've never heard a noise like this before.)
They're coming round again. And it's appalling –
The moment when you can't stand any more,
The Green Light goes! *Geronimo! Excelsior!*

It's Gangway for the New Apocalypse!
They're racing at two hundred miles an hour!
The likelier contenders get to grips
Like heavy cavalry berserk with power
And three-time-winner *Foyt* already rips
Away to lead the field by half a mile
As up the ante goes. Down go the chips.
No-one but *Rutherford* can match that style,
And he starts too far back. I'll tell you in a while

The way it all comes out, but now I've got
To set this screed aside and keep a check
From lap to lap on who, while driving what,
Gets hit by whom or ends up in a wreck.
A half a thousand miles is quite a trek –
Though even as I'm jotting down this line
A.J.'s got someone breathing down his neck . . .
Yes, *Rutherford*'s *MacLaren*, from Row Nine,
Has moved up more than twenty places. Heady wine!

Since *Johnny Rutherford* is from *Fort Worth*
And *Foyt* from *Houston*, they are *Texans* Twain:
The both of them behind the wheel since birth,
The both of them straight-arrow as *John Wayne*.
This thing they're doing's technically insane
And yet there's no denying it's a thrill:
For something fundamental in the brain
Rejoices in the daring and the skill.
The heart is lifted, even though the blood may chill.

It's SOME TIME LATER. On the Victory dais
Glad *Rutherford* gets kissed and plied with drink.
It looks a bit like supper at *Emmaus*.
Unceasing worship's damaging, I think:
One's standards of self-knowledge tend to sink.
I'd like to try it, though, I must confess.
Perhaps a little bit. Not to the brink.
Nor would that heap of lolly cause distress:
Three hundred thousand dollars – not a penny less.

Until half-way, the prize belonged to *Foyt*.
His pretty GILMORE RACING ketchup-red
Coyote skated flatter than a quoit,
The maestro lying down as if in bed.
He only led by inches, but he led –
Until his turbo-charger coughed white smoke.
The car kept running quickly while it bled,
But finally – Black Flag. For *Foyt*, no joke:
Unless he had his money on the other bloke.

The Coming Boy on his eleventh try
At winning the '500' finished First.
A perfect journey. No-one had to die.
On looking back, I think about the worst
Catastrophe was that an engine burst.

The empty *Brickyard* bakes in silent heat,
The quarter-million race-fans have dispersed,
And I have got a deadline I must meet:
I have to tell the story of the Champion's defeat.

Velazquez was ennobled in the end.
(Old *Philip*, fading fast, could not refuse
The final accolade to such a friend.)
His background was examined for loose screws
(Against the blood of craftsmen, *Moors* or *Jews*
Bureaucracy imposed a strict embargo)
And in a year or so came the good news,
Together with the robes and wealthy cargo
They used to hang around a *Knight of Santiago*.

Encumbered thus, he sank into the grave.
The Man is dead. The Artist is alive.
For lonely are the brilliant, like the brave –
Exactly like, except their deeds survive.
My point (it's taken ages to arrive)
Is simply this: enjoy the adulation,
But meanwhile take a tip from Uncle *Clive*
And *amplify your general education*.
There's more than Literature involved in Cultivation.

Tomorrow in the *London* afternoon
I'll miss your stubby, *Jaggerish* appearance
And wish you back in *Fleet Street* very soon.
Among the foremost ranks of your adherents
I'm vocal to the point of incoherence
When totting up your qualities of mind.
You've even got the rarest: Perseverance.
A wise adviser ought to be resigned,
Unless he keeps the pace hot, to being left behind.

'We're given Art in order not to perish
From the Truth.' Or words to that effect.
An apophthegm of *Nietzsche*'s which I cherish :
He sees how these two areas connect
Without conceding that they intersect.
Enough for now. Go easy, I implore you.
It all abides your questing intellect.
The Heritage of Culture, I assure you,
Like everything, you lucky sod, is All Before You.

TO PETE ATKIN:
A LETTER FROM PARIS

Trapped here in *Paris*, *Pete*, to shoot some scenes
Which end a film that's tied me up for weeks,
I've lost track of what what I'm doing means.
The streets of the *Étoile* are filled like creeks
By driving rain that blinds our fine machines.
We squat indoors, unprepossessing freaks
Made up as rough-cast hoboes of both sexes,
Surrounded by Sun-Guns and *Panaflexes*.

Our schedule's gone to *Hades*. Meanwhile you
Have gone to *Scotland*, there to make the rounds
Of Clubs and Halls to introduce our new
Collection of low-down yet highbrow sounds –
A sacrifice I hail. And so, in lieu
Of calls that would be tricky and cost pounds,
I'm scrawling you this missive in *ottava*,
A form I like like *Fields* liked *Mokka-Java*.

That *Byron* incarnates *Don Juan* in it
Should make it suicide to use again.
This note would end before I could begin it
Were I to dwell on that least pinched of men
(Who turned these stanzas out at two a minute)
And bring to mind the splendour of his pen,
The sheer *élan*, the lift, the loose-limbed jollity –
Yes, blue – but *true* blue, right? Legit. Star quality.

A strength that helps to prove these verse-form shapes
(Home-spun or else, like this one now, imported)
Are far from being decorative drapes
Deployed to prettify some ill-assorted
Conceptions best half-hidden : the gap gapes
Between the Thought and Deed (and drawn and quartered
Lies your result) if *that's* your estimation.
These strict schemes are a kind of cogitation

In their own right. Without them, no real thinking
Beyond the surface flotsam in the skull
Can happen. It takes more than steady drinking
To stop Creative Writers being dull.
Their gifts they'll soon find upside-down and sinking
If Discipline has not first keeled the hull.
For all true poets Rhyme must equal Reason
And Formlessness be just a form of Treason.

So no surprise you were the man for me,
Though others sang with much more cute a voice.
Approval was no matter of degree
But absolute. There was no other choice.
Our linking-up was pure Necessity,
As certainly as *Rolls* had need of *Royce*.
I viewed you, while the *Footlights* shouted Encore,
The way one *Goncourt* viewed the other *Goncourt*.

This kid, I mused, knows how to grasp the nettle.
With him the formal urge is automatic.
He's lamped the fact that only Heat moulds metal
Or Pressure makes the Lyrical dramatic.
One's syllables would soon attain fine fettle
If tethered to his notes, be less erratic;
One's lexical Pizzazz avoid fatuity
Attached to that melodic Perspicuity.

We met, we talked of *Bean* and *Brute* and *Bird*
And *Rabbit*. You were full of praise for *Trane*.
We both thought early *Miles* had had the Word
But (now I know this went against the grain)
I thought he later lost it. Had I heard
Of *Archie Shepp?* Yes. Good? No. Right : inane.
Our views were close, and on one salient thing
Inseparably united – *Duke* was King.

Of *Main Stem, 'C' Jam Blues* and *Cottontail*,
Of *Take the 'A' Train, In a Mellotone*
And *Harlem Air Shaft* we took turns to wail
The solos so definitively blown
By sidemen somewhere in the Age of Sail –
The pre-war *Forties*, when *Duke* stood alone,
His every disc a miniature immensity,
The acme of schooled ease and spacious density.

It soon turned out you thought post-*Presley* Pop
As real as Jazz. This wheeze was new to me
And caught my sense of fitness on the hop :
I loved the stuff, but come now, *seriously* . . .
Hold on, though. My beliefs howled to a stop
And chose reverse. With one bound, Jack was free.
Did Rock strike me as flexible and lively? Good.
Then why not get in there and gain a livelihood?

The *Broadway* partnership of Words and Tune
Had been dissolved by Pop, which then reverted
In all good faith to rhyming *Moon* with *June*,
Well pleased with the banalities it blurted.
Those speech defects would need attention soon.
Gillespie and *Kildare*, in aim concerted,
We got started . . . but enough now in that strain :
The whole a.m. has just gone down the drain.

I'm sure the cost of sitting here is frightening
And days ago it ceased to be much fun.
Though, as we lunch, the sky might just be lightening:
This afternoon we could get something done.
And now the outlook's *definitely* brightening,
So more from the location. I must run.
We've just been told to grab a cab and ride out
To some guy called *Quatorze*'s country hideout.

* *

The weather's cleared. We're filming at *Versailles*,
Palatial residence of Sun-King *Louis*,
Where everything is landscaped save the sky
And even that seems strangely free of *pluie*
For this one day at least. I find that I
Am sneakily inclined to murmur 'phooey'
When faced with all this Classical Giganticism:
In fact it almost makes me like Romanticism.

Proportion, yes: the joint's got that to burn.
Sa regularity of window arch,
Ses ranks of cornucopia and urn.
Those balustrades like soldiers on the march!
Those gardens, haunt of robot coot and hern!
The whole confection fairly reeks of starch:
A dude-ranch frozen with neurotic tension,
It chills the very notion of Dissension.

And that was what *le Roi Soleil* was after,
Without a doubt. His Absolutist frown
Is there in every pediment and rafter,
A stare of disapproval beating down
Propensities to any form of laughter
Beyond the courtly Hollow kind. The Crown
Made sure to keep this 4-star barracks filled
With dupes who thought they danced but really drilled.

Grim-jawed Solemnity may have its worth
But Geniality is just as serious
And *gravitas* is half-deaf without Mirth.
I don't mean one should roll around delirious
But Art must take the air, not hug the earth –
Authoritative needn't mean Imperious.
To preach cold concepts like the Golden Section
Is over-mightily to seek Perfection.

We should be glad, then, that we work in Rock
Whose mark for ordered Symmetry is Zero.
Its *cognoscenti*, talking total cock
Concerning slack-mouthed bitch or dildoed hero,
Combine the thickness of a Mental Block
With all the musicality of *Nero*:
And yet despite their I.Q.'s in two figures
They've sussed out where the only decent gig is.

In liking Anti-Intellectualism
They're wrong, but right to value simple Verve.
A long way gone in pale Eclecticism,
Like all those nostrums that no longer serve
(*Vendanta, Joan the Wad, Collectivism*)
The Classical Succession's lost its nerve –
Or else it shrieks an *avant-gardiste* foolery
That makes the average Rock Song shine like joolery.

But here the shine's gone off a hard half-day:
We're wrapping up with no shots left to do.
Inside a camera-car I'm borne away
Along a six-lane speedway to *St Cloud*,
Where signboards set to lead non-Frogs astray
Now send us back *Versailles*-wards. Sacray bloo.
Our pub will keep a meal, though . . . Bloody Hell!
No food: we have to work *tonight* as well.

* *

Throughout the evening's shooting in *Pigalle*
I marvel, as the red lights glow infernally,
That they can pull down places like *Les Halles*
When (rain or shine, nocturnally, diurnally,
Uncaring if you snigger, sneer or snarl)
Grim tat and tit dance cheek by jowl eternally
In *this* dump. What a drag! But it's survival
Is no surprise if *Taste*'s its only rival.

Alone at last, I'm much too tired to sleep
(A hemistitch from *Lorenz Hart*. You tumbled?)
The drapes down-soft, the wall-to-wall knee-deep,
My hotel bedroom ought to leave me humbled.
By rights I should conk out without a peep,
But can't. The boys who did the *décor* fumbled:
It's just too scrumptious to be borne, too peachy.
They've ladled on an acre too much chi-chi.

The *Gauche* and not the *Droite*'s the *Rive* for me.
To kip beneath plush quilts is not the same
As gazing *sur les toits* of that Paree
They fly behind the garret window-frame,
Heraldic as France Ancient's *fleur-de-lys*,
To charm you through Act 1 of *La Bohème* –
Unless I've got *Parnasse* mixed up with *Martre*.
(You know I *still* can't tell those *Monts* apartre?)

So much for *Taste*, then, and the same goes double
For those more recent phantoms, such as *Youth*.
As clear and brilliant as the tiny bubble
That canopies a baby's first front tooth,
There swells through times of sloth and troughs of trouble
The Artist's one eternal, guiding Truth –
Ars longa, vita brevis. Is that *Horace*?
It could be someone weird, like *William Morris*.

* *

I'm writing half-way up the *Eiffel Tower*
While knocking back a rich *café au lait.*
We've been at work this high about an hour
And here my part will end, at Noon today.
It gives a heady, *Zeus*-like sense of power
To watch, from *au-dessus de la mêlée,*
The myriad formiculant mere mortals
Who circumvest this crazy structure's portals.

Much earlier, and lovely in the Dawn,
The gardens of the *Louvre* were full of mist.
The *Tuileries* lay like a smoking lawn
As I, my trusty notebook in my fist,
Saw *Paris* come unfolded like a fawn
And glitter like a powdered amethyst –
Whereat I felt, involved in her fragility,
A thumping streak of Tough Bitch durability.

We're all aware of how the Continuity
Of Western Culture's frazzled to a thread.
It doesn't take a soothsayer's acuity
To see the whole shebang might wind up dead.
One's sorely tempted to, in perpetuity,
Give up the struggle and go back to bed:
And yet TRADITION, though we can't renew it,
Demands we add our Certain Something to it

No matter what. I leave from *Charles de Gaulle*
At *Roissy* this p.m. S-F HQ!
The planes feed in a cluster, like a shoal
Of mutant carp stuck nose to nose with glue
Around a doughnut in whose abstract hole
Aphasic humans escalating through
Translucent pipelines linking zones to domes
Seem pastel genes in giant chromosomes.

And that's the Future, baby. Like the Past
It's flowing, but unlike it it flows faster.
Ici Paris, below me. Will it last?
A heap of ageing bricks and wood and plaster –
Bombe glacée with one atomic blast.
A single finger's tremble from disaster.
But then, who isn't? So what else is new?
See you in *London*: there's a lot to do.

TO PRUE SHAW:
A LETTER FROM CAMBRIDGE

I miss you. As I settle down to write,
   Creating for my forearm room to rest,
   I see the hard grey winter evening light
Is scribbled-on with lipstick in the West
   As just another drowsy *Cambridge* day
   Discreetly shines and shyly looks its best
Before, with eyeballs glazed, it slides away
   And slips into a night's sleep deeper still,
   Where *Morpheus* holds undisputed sway
Throughout the weary academic mill –
   An atmosphere of cosy somnolence
   I hope that I can summon up the will
To counteract. I'm striving to condense
   Within the *terza rima* my ideas
   Concerning us, the Arts and World Events.
I shake my skull, which for the moment clears,
   And shape a line to say that minus you
   I'm lonelier than *Hell* and bored to tears:
Then slumber paints my eyelids thick with glue.
   Uncertainty bemuses. Somewhere round
   Lake Garda you've got lost and left no clue.
The post is void of cards, the phone of sound.
   If you were elsewhere than in *Italy*
   I'd start a hue and cry to get you found,
But as things are I think it best to be
   More circumspect. The blower's on the blink
   Across the strike-bound North from sea to sea,
And *Heaven* only knows the waste of ink

Involved in trusting letters to the mail.
The Ship of State is getting set to sink
Again. (The poor thing never learned to sail.)
   Italia! Poverina! Yes, and yet
The place's old enchantments never fail
To work their subtle wiles. You'll not forget,
   I'm sure, when passing ice-cold *Sirmione*,
   The way we used to swim and not get wet
In water soft and warm as *zabaglione*.
   The titles to the olive groves and palaces
   Catullus walked with courtesan and crony
In our time were *Onassis*'s and *Callas*'s
   But as you stood hip-deep in liquid air
   I thought the moment sweet past all analysis
And thanked the pagan Gods I knew were there
   (The sunset stretched a ladder of gold chains
   Across the lake) that they'd been so unfair
In handing you the beauty *and* the brains.
   An egocentric monster then as now
   I graciously resolved to keep my gains
By staying near you, never thinking how
   You might not co-divide that deep esteem.
   Unwarrantedly dry of palm and brow
I wed you, in due course. Today I dream
   Of what I would, if I had missed the boat
   Undoubtedly have undergone. A scream
Of retroactive anguish rends my throat.
   That physicist from *Stockholm* you refused,
   The one who tried to buy you a fur coat:
To think of the affection I abused!
   Now here was this attractive, well-heeled bloke,
   Whose talk of synchrotrons kept you amused,
Whose china-white *Mercedes* – Holy Smoke!
   What made me certain he should get the grief
   And I the joy? I swear I almost croak
From apprehension mingled with relief

46

Recalling how I flirted with defeat.
It's only now I think myself a thief –
Of his luck and your time. You were to meet
Yet brighter prospects later. I still won.
I had a system nobody could beat.
I flailed about and called my folly fun
For years and even then was not too late:
The threads that joined us were as strongly spun
As your forgivingness of me was great.
I wonder that your heart has not grown numb,
So long you've had (or felt you've had) to wait
For my unthinking fondness to become
A love for you like yours for me. The fault
Is all mine if it has, for being dumb.
I'd have no comeback under *Heaven*'s vault
– my only plea could be *è colpa mia*,
A hanging head, and tears that tasted salt –
If you should fade from my life like *la Pia*.
But you have not, so I shall for the nonce
Eschew this droning form of logorrhoea
Which feeds upon what might have happened once
And hasten to give thanks that you and I,
Like *Verdi* and *Strepponi* or the *Lunts*,
Seem apt, so far at least, to give the lie
To notions that all order falls apart –
Though giving them as one who would defy
The Gods, yet feels a flutter in his heart.
Has something happened? Down there, so much can.
The Right Wing terrorists are acting smart.
They've thought hard and have come up with a Plan:
To bomb the innocent. Earmarked for death
Are woman, daughter, child and unarmed man.
From now on no-one draws an easy breath.
Your train ride down to *Florence* will be like
Accepting a night's lodging from *Macbeth*.
I wonder if you'd rather hire a bike?

Except the roads aren't safe. Well, why not walk?
    You'd thrive on a four hundred mile hike . . .
But no, all this is Fearful Husband's talk:
    What-might-be acting like what-might-have-been
    To turn my knees to jelly, cheeks to chalk.
No matter how Infernal the Machine
    Prepared to blow our sheltered lives to bits,
    It would be less than just, indeed obscene,
To harbour the suspicion murder fits
    The Italian National Character. Not so.
    As always, most of them live by their wits
Amidst – as, to your cost, you've come to know –
    Administrative chaos. It's a wonder
    That utter barbarism's been so slow
In gaining ground from brouhaha and blunder,
    Yet even when *Fascismo* had its hour
    The blood was always upstaged by the thunder.
They held pyjama parties with their power
    Forgetting to wipe out a single race.
    Some blockhead said a bomb was like a flower,
Some Communists got booted in the face,
    But no-one calls that lapse a Holocaust –
    More like a Farce that ended in disgrace,
When men yelled like a racing car's exhaust
    In uniforms adorned with a toy dagger;
    A time when word and meaning were divorced,
Divided by a verbal strut and swagger
    As pompous as a moose's mating-call,
    Bombastic as a war-dance by *Mick Jagger*.
But we both know it's not like that at all,
    The eternal *Italy*, the one that matters.
    The blue-chinned heavies at the costume ball
Whose togs inept explosions blow to tatters
    Are just the international tribe of jerks
    That crop up anywhere, as mad as hatters,
To pistol-whip the poor and cop the perks.

The real Italians, far from on the make,
Are makers. Ye shall know them by their works –
To which the guide who brought me wide awake
    Was you, ten years ago. You were my tutor.
    At times you must have thought this a mistake
And wished me elsewhere, or at least astuter.
    I paced our tiny rented room in *Rome*,
    I crackled like an overtaxed computer
And used my nerve-wracked fingers for a comb,
    Attempting to construe *Inferno* Five.
    It took so long I wanted to go home
But comprehension started to arrive
    At last. I saw the lovers ride the storm
    And felt the pulse which brought the dead alive.
For sheer intensity of lyric form
    I'd never read that stretch of verse's peer.
    You said such things, with *Dante*, were the norm.
You proved it, as we read on for a year.
    And so it was our *Galahad*, that book,
    As well as one ordained to make it clear
How Art and Intellect are king and rook
    And not just man and wife and guest and host –
    They link together like an eye and hook
While each moves through the other like a ghost.
    Both interpenetrate inside the mind
    And, in creation, nothing matters most –
By *Dante* these great facts are underlined,
    Made incandescent like a sunlit rose.
    My clenched fist thumped my forehead. I'd been blind!
Awaking from a *Rip Van Winkle* doze
    I realized I'd been groping in the gloom,
    Not even good at following my nose.
A knowing bride had schooled a clumsy groom:
    Belated, crude, but strong, his urge to learn
    Began there, in that shoe-box of a room –
A classic eager dim-wit doomed to burn

The candle at both ends while, head in hands,
He mouths what he can only just discern
And paragraphs twice read half understands.
    To *Petrarch*'s verses and to *Croce*'s thought
    We moved on later. Etiquette demands
I don't go on about the books we bought
    In all those second-hand shops we infested.
    I've never mastered grammar as I ought.
My scraps of erudition aren't Digested.
    But still I've grown, drawn out by what I've read,
    More cosmopolitan – well, less sequestered.
(Our old friend *Goethe*, writing in his head,
    Would tap out stresses on his girlfriend's spine.
    Gorblimey, talk about Technique in Bed!
Urbanity on *that* scale's not my line.
    I must admit, however, that at times
    I found my brain, as well as fogged with wine,
Inopportunely chattering with rhymes.)
    And then there were the canvases and frescoes,
    Cascading like a visual change of chimes
Or stacked ten-deep like racks of tins in *Tesco*'s
    All over *Rome* and *Naples*, *Florence*, *Venice* . . .
    I felt like a research group of UNESCO's
Investigating some microbic menace:
    To sort it out, life wasn't long enough.
    It just went on like *Rosewall* playing tennis.
There wasn't any end to all that stuff.
    An early *Raphael*, or late *Perugino*?
    (I haven't got a clue. I'll have to bluff.)
Who sculpted this, *Verrocchio* or *Mino*?
    (But who the heck was *Mino*?) No doubt what
    The banquet would have soon become (a beano
With sickness as the sequel) had you not
    Been there to function as my dietitian;
    Ensuring I'd not try to scoff the lot
But merely taste each phase at its fruition,

Assimilating gradually, and thus
Catch up with *Europe*'s Civilized Tradition –
Which wasn't really a departing bus,
    You argued, but a spirit all around me
    I'd get attuned to if I didn't fuss.
From that time forward every summer found me
    In *Florence*, where you studied all year long.
    Your diligence continued to astound me.
I went on getting attributions wrong,
    But bit by bit I gained perceptiveness
    As day by day I keenly helped to throng
The galleries, exalted – nothing less –
    By how those fancy lads all worked like slaves
    To make their age so howling a Success
Before they rolled, fulfilled, into their graves.
    In *Cambridge*, night wears on. The evening ending
    Will soon dictate the sleep my system craves.
I'll close. These lines might just be worth the sending
    To *Florence*, care of *Rita* at her flat.
    Supposing they get through, they'll wait there, pending
Your safe arrival – and amen to that.
    That city is a place where we were poor.
    In furnished dungeons blacker than your hat
We slept, or failed to, on the concrete floor
    And met the morning's heat chilled to the bone –
    Yet each day we felt better than before
Forgetting what it meant to be alone.
    Well, this is what it means : distracting games
    With tricky rhyme-schemes and – wait, there's the phone.
'Will you accept a call from *Mrs. James*?'
    P.S. You've made this letter obsolete
    But rather than consign it to the flames
I'll send it. For you must admit, my sweet,
    A triple-rhyming verse communication,
    While scarcely ranking as an epic feat,
Deserves perusal by its Inspiration.

51

TO TOM STOPPARD:
A LETTER FROM LONDON

To catch your eye in *Paris, Tom*,
I choose a show-off stanza from
   Some *Thirties* play
Forgotten now like *Rin Tin Tin*.
Was it '*The Dog beneath the skin*'?
   Well, anyway

Its tone survives. The metres move
Through Time like paintings in the *Louvre*
   (Say loov, not loover):
Coherent in their verbal jazz,
They're confident of tenure as
   J. Edgar Hoover.

Pink Fairies of the Sixth Form Left,
Those Ruined Boys at least were deft
   At the actual Writing.
Though History scorns all they thought,
The nifty artefacts they wrought
   Still sound exciting.

Distinguishing the higher fliers
Remorselessly from plodding triers
   Who haven't got it,
Such phonic zip bespeaks a knack
Of which no labour hides the lack:
   A child could spot it.

And boy, you've got the stuff in bales –
A *Lubitsch*-Touch that never fails.
     The other guys
Compared to you write lines that float
With all the grace of what gets wrote
     By *Ernest Wise*.

The *Stoppard* dramaturgic moxie
Unnerves the priests of orthodoxy:
     We still hear thicks
Who broadcast the opinion freely
Your plays are Only Sketches Really –
     Just bags of tricks.

If dramas do not hammer Themes
Like pub bores telling you their dreams
     The dense don't twig.
They want the things they know already
Reiterated loud and steady –
     Drilled through the wig.

From all frivolity aloof,
Those positivist killjoys goof
     Two ways at once:
They sell skill short, and then ignore
The way your works are so much more
     Than clever stunts.

So frictionless a *jeu d'esprit*,
Like *Wittgenstein*'s philosophy,
     Appears to leave
Things as they are, but at the last
The Future flowing to the Past
     Without reprieve

Endorses everything you've done.
As *Einstein* puts it, The Old One
  Does Not Play Dice,
And though your gift might smack of luck
Laws guide it, like the hockey puck
  Across the ice.

Deterministic you are not,
However, even by a jot.
  Your sense of form
Derives its casual power to thrill
From operating at the still
  Heart of the storm.

For how could someone lack Concern
Who cared that gentle *Guildenstern*
  And *Rosencrantz*
(Or else the same names rearranged
Should those two men be interchanged)
  Were sent by Chance

To meet a death at *Hamlet*'s whim
Less grand than lay in store for him,
  But still a death :
A more appalling death, in fact
Than any King's in the Fifth Act –
  Even *Macbeth*?

In *South-East Asia* as I type
The carbuncle is growing ripe
  Around *Saigon*.
The citadels are soon reduced.
The chickens have come home to roost.
  The heat is on,

And we shall see a sickness cured
Which virulently has endured
    These thirty years:
The torturers ran out of jails,
The coffin-makers out of nails,
    Mothers of tears,

While all the Furies and the Fates
Unleashed by the *United States*
    In Freedom's name
Gave evidence that moral error
Returns in tumult and in terror
    The way it came.

But now the conquerors bring Peace.
When *everyone* is in the police
    There's no unrest.
Except for those who disappear
The People grin from ear to ear –
    Not like the *West*.

Rejecting both kinds of belief
(Believing only in the grief
    Their clash must bring)
We find to use the words we feel
Adhere most closely to the Real
    Means everything.

I like the kind of jokes you tell
And what's more you like mine as well –
    Clear proof of nous.
I like your stylish way of life.
I've thought of kidnapping your wife.
    I like your house.

Success appeals to my sweet tooth :
But finally it's to the Truth
   That you defer –
And that's the thing I like the best.
My love to *Miri*. Get some rest.
   A tout à l'heure.

TO PETER PORTER:
A LETTER TO SYDNEY

To reach you in the *You-Beaut Country, Peter,*
Perforce I choose that scheme of rhyme and metre
Most favoured by your master spirit, *Pope* –
Whose pumiced forms make mine look like soft soap,
Despite the fact that this last fiscal year
Two thousand of my couplets, pretty near,
Have been read out in public – a clear token
The Classical Tradition's not yet broken,
Just mangled and left twitching in a ditch
By *Aussies* apt to scratch the fatal itch
That *Juvenal* and *Dr Johnson* dubbed
Cacoethes scribendi and well drubbed.
Your friends in *London* miss you something fierce:
You are the crux of talk like *Mildred Pierce.*
At *Mille Pini* or in *Bertorelli's*
We scriveners still meet to stoke our bellies
And with red wine we toast you *in absentia*
From soup to nuts and so on to dementia.
The grape-juice flowing in across our dentures,
Tall tales flow out concerning your adventures.
As fleet of foot and fearless as *Phidippides*
You are our pioneer in the *Antipodes,*
A latter-day but no less dauntless *Jason*
Or *Flying Dutchman* as played by *James Mason.*
Vespucci, Tasman, Drake, Cook, Scott, John Glenn –
To those you left behind you're all these men:
The Town's not heard such daydreams of bravado
Since *Raleigh* sailed in search of *El Dorado.*

One rumour says that cheap drinks on the plane
Had detrimental impact on your brain:
It's said you smiled a smile like *Nat King Cole*'s
While trying to take over the controls.
Another rumour graphically describes
The shameless way they're plying you with bribes
(A Philistine approach we're sure you'll spurn)
To make your trip a permanent return.
They've offered you £10,000 a year,
We're told, to dwell Out There instead of here –
Plus car, two yachts, a house at *Double Bay*
And *Mrs Whitlam* in a negligée.
Temptation! You'd not only soon get rich,
Your kids would scarcely need to wear a stitch –
They'd be as brown as berries in two shakes.
Perhaps you *ought* to up stakes for *their* sakes . . .
To let them share the unexampled wealth
Australia's Young are given free – Good Health.
Good Health (i.e., preventive pediatrics)
Provides the punch behind *Jeff Thomson*'s hat-tricks.
Good Health ensures the *Ashes* stay Down Under.
It lends *John Newcombe*'s smashes extra thunder.
Good Health is what puts beefcake on *Rod Taylor* –
It makes *Rolf Harris* sound like a loud-hailer.
Good Health helps *Eddie Charlton* score like *Bradman*
And *Sidney Nolan* sling paint like a madman.
But vitamins and body-building cereals
Are only some among the raw materials
That go to stuff the bulging cornucopia
Which all wise men now know to be *Utopia* –
Though once none but the hopeless ever went there
And Death was preferable to being sent there.
The tables are well turned. The biter's bitten.
The Pit of Desperation now is *Britain* –
Where soon must fall a Dark Night of the Soul
With (HEALEY WARNS) Three Million On The Dole

Unless some pin is found to pierce inflation
And thereby save the Pound and thus the Nation.
For their own chances loth to give you tuppence,
The *British* seem concussed by their come-uppance:
Like fearful *Pooh* and *Piglet* they keep humming,
But few believe a cure will be forthcoming
That won't make their poor country even poorer –
A bald man getting drunk on hair-restorer.
To say 'So much the better' would be base
As well as out of key and not my place,
And yet, though some might deem the pause a pity,
The Slump seems to have saved our favourite City
From being hacked to pieces like *King Priam*'s –
Here by *Joe Levy*, there by *Harry Hyams*.
May wasting assets pauperize them both:
They made a graveyard and they called it Growth.
But now it's clear (thank *Heaven* for small mercies)
The Land Boom was a siren-song like *Circe*'s
That sapped the system's last remaining vigour
By crooning 'You must go on getting bigger'.
To which thought there can only be one answer –
A flagrant *Harvey Smith*, for so must Cancer.
Forgive me if that reference to pathology
Offends your deep concern with Eschatology –
The Last Things are for you no laughing matter
And there I go reducing them to patter.
You think of Death, you've told me, all the time,
And not as a quietus but a crime.
You think of Death, you've told me, as a curse
That caps a life of pain with something worse.
You think of Death, you've told me, as obscene,
And all your poems show me what you mean,
For your horrific vision would make *Goya*
Plead mental cruelty and phone his lawyer –
And even *Dürer*'s '*Ritter, Tod und Teufel*'
Beside what you evoke looks almost joyful.

A paradox, in view of this, that you,
Of all the *London* Literary crew,
Are much the most authentically elated
By everything Great Artists have created.
I miss your talk not just because of savouring
Its bracing lack of artificial flavouring,
But also for the way that *Grub Street* scandal
Is spiced by you with thoughts on *Bach* and *Handel*,
And whether the true high-point of Humanity
Was *Mozart*'s Innocence or *Haydn*'s Sanity.
For though your calling's Poetry, your passion
Is MUSIC – and I'm cast in the same fashion,
Believing that Man's Fate, if hardly cherishable,
Through MUSIC may partake of the Imperishable.
(A sacrament, I fear, which smacks of heresy
To some of our close friends among the clerisy,
Who can't conceive of anybody needing it –
And stick to writing Verse, while rarely reading it.)
Enough. Since this must reach you through the *'Staggers'*
Claire Tomalin will look askance and daggers
At claims for space beyond a second column,
So I shall close. Perhaps with something solemn?
Alas, I'm ill-equipped for sounding cryptic.
Besides, I just don't feel Apocalyptic!
For all her empty coffers ring like cisterns,
For all her strength now lies with *Sonny Liston*'s,
For all her looming Future looks appalling,
GREAT BRITAIN must for always be enthralling
To anyone who speaks her native tongue.
Turn back, and leave *Australia* to the Young!
Turn back, and push a pencil as you ought!
Turn back! The times are right for rhymed report!
We need you here to help us face the Crunch
(Or, failing that, to face the bill for lunch),
Lest in these islands Folly govern men
Until the day *King Arthur* comes again –

And finds, no doubt, his advent greeted warmly
by *Jack Jones, Arthur Scargill* and *Joe Gormley.*